Lincoln Peirce

BiG NATE
LAUGH-O-RAMA

HarperCollins *Children's Books*

Also by Lincoln Peirce

Big Nate: The Boy with the Biggest Head in the World
Big Nate Strikes Again
Big Nate on a Roll
Big Nate Goes for Broke
Big Nate: Boredom Buster
Big Nate: Fun Blaster
Big Nate: What Could Possibly Go Wrong?
Big Nate: Here Goes Nothing!
Big Nate Flips Out
Big Nate: Doodlepalooza
Big Nate: Genius Mode
Big Nate in the Zone
Big Nate: Mr Popularity

First published in Great Britain by HarperCollins *Children's Books* in 2014.
HarperCollins *Children's Books* is a division of HarperCollins*Publishers*
Ltd, 77-85 Fulham Palace Road, Hammersmith, London, W6 8JB.

www.harpercollins.co.uk

2

Text and illustrations © 2014 United Feature Syndicate, Inc.

ISBN 978-0-00-756907-6

The author asserts the moral right to be identified as
the author of this work.

Printed and bound in England by Clays Ltd, St Ives plc.

For Big Nate Fans All Over the World –
Especially if you love…
cartooning,
laugh attacks,
Cheez Doodles,
scribble games, and
green beans (OK, forget that last one.)

POP QUIZ PARTY!

Are you a Big Nate know-it-all? Prove it!

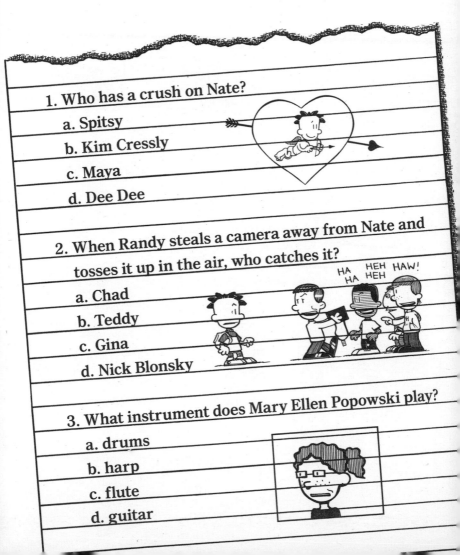

1. Who has a crush on Nate?

    a. Spitsy

    b. Kim Cressly

    c. Maya

    d. Dee Dee

2. When Randy steals a camera away from Nate and tosses it up in the air, who catches it?

    a. Chad

    b. Teddy

    c. Gina

    d. Nick Blonsky

    HA HEH HAW!
    HA HEH

3. What instrument does Mary Ellen Popowski play?

    a. drums

    b. harp

    c. flute

    d. guitar

4. This is Gina's Trivia Slam team name.

a. Gina's Gorgeous Brains

b. Gina's Gonna Get You

c. Gina's Geniuses

d. Gina's Great Gamers

5. Francis DOESN'T do this:

a. colour code his underwear

b. iron his tube socks

c. speak in baby talk to his cat

d. get a C on his homework

BONUS POINTS!

When Uncle Pedro hypnotises Nate, he becomes. . .

a. funnier

b. a world-class guitarist

c. neat

d. a hip-hop dancer

(Hint: Use the secret code

on page 9!)

TO THE RESCUE!

Never fear, Ultra-Nate is here!! Fill in the speech bubbles and decide how he saves the day!

GOTCHA!

Have you ever had a bad-picture day? Take a look at these silly shots! Make up a crazy caption for each one.

_____

_____

_____

_____

NOW DRAW YOUR OWN
<u>WEIRDEST</u> PHOTOS EVER!

YOU

YOUR BEST FRIEND

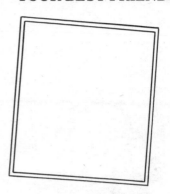

YOUR TEACHER

_____

(fill in the blank)

ALL WE'RE SAYING IS, THERE'S SOMETHING **FUNNY** ABOUT EMBARRASSING PICTURES!

WALK THE PLANK

Nate's friend Chad wears his favourite pirate hat during the Trivia Slam showdown. How well do you know pirates? Try this puzzler and see!

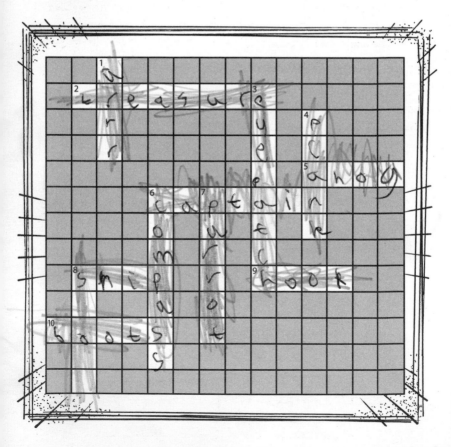

CLUES

ACROSS

2. The glistening gold and jewels that pirates seek.

5. How pirates say "Hello!" It rhymes with "boy."

6. The leader of the sailors.

8. A vessel that travels on the high seas.

9. A replacement for a pirate's hand; rhymes with "cook."

10. Tall, brown, and leather, these will keep your feet warm.

DOWN

1. What pirates say when they're angry; the last three letters are the same.

3. A black accessory that covers one of your eyes.

4. A wooden board that rhymes with "sank." Walk the _____.

6. This will lead you to true North.

7. Feathered friend that often sits atop one's shoulder; rhymes with "carrot."

8. Long and sharp, this weapon serves pirates in battle.

NAME THAT BRAIN!

Test your Big Nate know-how! Match each character with their favourite subjects – draw a line from each set of subjects to the right character.

science fiction, martial arts, video games	GINA HEMPHILL-TOMS
sports, comedy, foreign languages, movie quotes	ERIC FLEURY
NO INFO	DEE DEE HOLLOWAY
art, drama, fashion, musical theatre	TEDDY ORTIZ
  every-thing ...and MORE!	? ? ? ?

CODE
CRACKER

Use this alphabet to decode the secret messages in this book. But don't show it to anybody else!

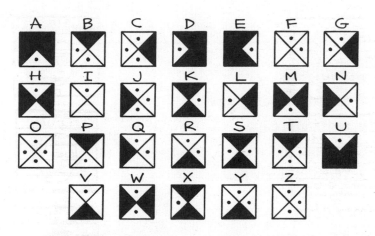

SECRET AGENT

Nate's dramatic friend Dee Dee loves playing a spy! Now you try. Decide what your secret spy identity will be. Circle your choices below.

SPY NAME: _____005_____

(You choose!)

DISGUISE:

a. moustache and beret ✓

b. mask and cape

c. glasses and wig

d. Halloween costume

THE **WHAT**? DEE DEE, WHAT ARE YOU **DOING**?

SIDEKICK:

a. your dog ✓

b. the pizza-delivery boy

c. a karate master

d. your crush

I'M GOING TO *SPY* ON **RANDY BET—**

SECRET SYMBOL:

a. star and moon

b. lightning flash

c. diamond in a circle

d. an *X* in a square ✓

NOW DRAW
YOURSELF IN YOUR
SPY DISGUISE!
(SHHH! DON'T TELL!)

SLAM DUNK

Who is the trivia champ of P.S. 38?

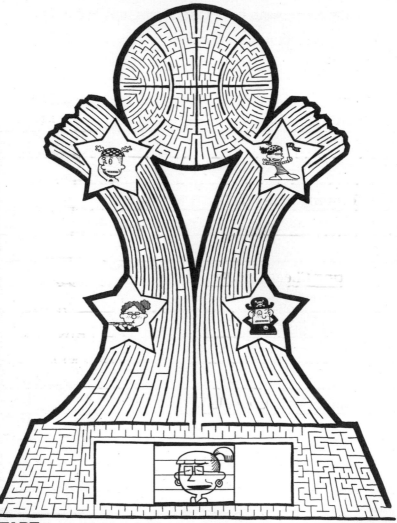

HALL MONITOR

Nate can't stand Nick Blonsky, the hall monitor who always reports him. List 15 reasons Nate gets into trouble, then rank them from 1 (no sweat) to 5 (worst ever).

REASON	RANK
1.	____
2.	____
3. Running in the hall	____
4.	____
5.	____
6. Eating Cheez Doodles	____
7.	____
8. No hall pass	____
9.	____
10.	____
11. Skateboarding inside	____
12.	____
13.	____
14.	____
15.	____

UGH. NICK.

WHAT ARE YOU DOING HERE?

DRESS TO IMPRESS

THERE'S NOTHING I ADORE MORE...

OOF!

Dee Dee is a fan of fabulous outfits! Find all the clothing and accessories in the word scramble on the opposite page and help Dee Dee get dressed!

HEADBAND

SNEAKERS

DIAMOND TIARA

NECKLACES

COWBOY HAT

RAINBOW BLOUSE

SATIN GLOVES

VEST

FEATHER BOA

LEG WARMERS

EARRINGS

STRIPED SCARF

SKIRT

ARGYLE SOCKS

```
F N K O F L R D P A O S S Y H G
E O C Q B Q T D G A N H E S I N
A I M Y I Y A D L Q I Q M F L V
T N A G S O T X E A R R I N G S
H A R G Y L E S O C K S Y E E V
E O A F M T A H Y O B W O C N N
R A I N B O W B L O U S E K H Q
B S T R I P E D S C A R F L R B
O N D S J E A R D N A B D A E H
A E N A E C F G H E E R L C A K
R A O W D V H E M O J S O E P T
S K M A O B N O S I K K H S C E
A E A N S E V O L G N I T A S E
D R I S I M L E G W A R M E R S
N S D R Q N O S M E G T S P B I
N Y O S M L C U Z T C E L A E S
```

I'VE GOT ANOTHER **FABULOUS** OUTFIT PLANNED!

WILD WORDS

Teddy and Francis combined the words "slob" and "pig" to make up a new word, "SLIG"!

NOW YOU TRY:

slime + dirty =

~~slitty~~

phobia + fright =

~~srobia~~

dumb + chuckle =

~~duckle~~

yellow + purple =

Yurple

stinky + old =

stold

yummy + fun =

Summy

SO FUNNY!

style + snappy =

Styley

spice + tasty =

Spastey

crazy + dork =

crork

SHORTCUT!

Nate knows a secret shortcut through Little Woods to get home from school. Check out Ms Clarke's lesson, then turn the page to create an awesome Mad Lib about your adventure in Little Woods!

Let's review the parts of speech. What is a noun?

A noun is a person, place, or thing.

EXAMPLES:

Mrs Godfrey (person), library (place), Book of Facts (thing)

EXAMPLES: memorise, practise, compete

EXAMPLES:

phony (Gina's smile)

snappy (Nate's comebacks)

dorky (Dee Dee's thinking caps)

MAKE A LIST OF THE COOLEST
WORDS YOU CAN THINK OF:

1. Noun:
2. Noun:
3. Verb:
4. Noun:
5. Plural noun:
6. Adjective:
7. Adjective:
8. Verb:
9. Noun:
10. Noun:
11. Noun:
12. Noun:
13. Noun:
14. Verb:
15. Noun:
16. Adjective:
17. Verb:
18. Verb:

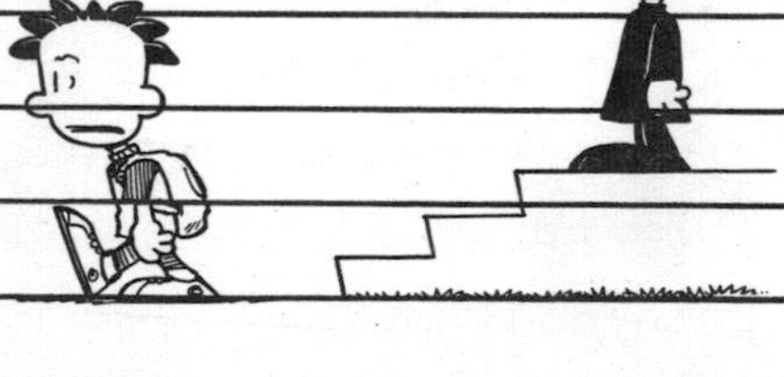

NOW FILL IN THE BLANKS
TO CREATE YOUR ADVENTURE!

When I enter the woods, I hear a _Ray_
1.

and trip on a _vine_, causing me to
2.

fall over quickly. As I turn up the hill, a
3.

bear drops out of a tree and lands on
4.

my _parkparle_. There are _wols_
5.   6.

noises all around, and I feel _scared_.
7.

I turn to _run_ when suddenly a
8.

Alex is in my path.
9.

"What's going on?" I think as I pick up the

___pack pack___ and put it in my ___back___.
10.   11.

I sigh and run towards the ___fire___
                                                            12.

when I see a ___monkey___ through the
                                              13.

clearing.

I ___shout___ loudly and sprint before
        14.

the ___monkey___ catches up. The sky turns
                  15.

___Blue___, and I ___ran___ through
  16.   17.

the mud and ___eraped___ as fast as I can!
                            18.

22

PROBLEM PICS!

Has your school picture ever turned out <u>TOTALLY</u>
terrible? Match each disaster to the right photo!

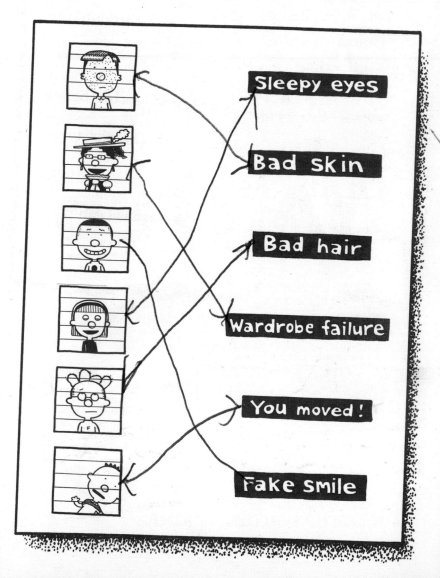

WANTED!

In *Big Nate Flips Out*, Nate suspects that sneaky Nick Blonsky stole the school camera. Draw your own WANTED posters for these characters and list their crimes. Are they too annoying? Or overly dramatic? You decide!

MAKE UP DEE DEE'S CRIME!

DECIDE NATE'S CRIME!

WHAT DID RANDY DO?

YOU'RE AN ACE!

Can you fill in the grid so that each card suit only appears once in every row, column, and box?

H = **HEART**

S = **SPADE**

C = **CLUB**

D = **DIAMOND**

MASTERMIND MATCH-UP

It's Trivia Slam time at P.S. 38, and Nate's ready for a showdown! Match each of his classmates to their trivia speciality!

every-
thing

comics,
Ben Franklin,
history of
snack foods,
Greek myths

flute
music,
cosmetology,
reality
television

breakfast,
scouting,
lunch,
animals,
dinner

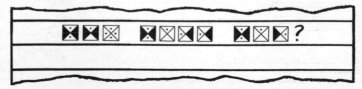

He's amazing, he's great, he's Ultra-Nate!
Fill in the speech bubbles and finish the story!

FACTASTIC FRANCIS

How well do <u>you</u> know Nate's best friend Francis??
Test your facts with this quick quiz!

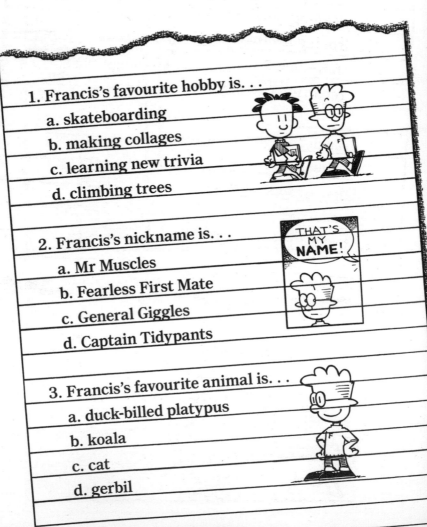

1. Francis's favourite hobby is. . .
   a. skateboarding
   b. making collages
   c. learning new trivia
   d. climbing trees

2. Francis's nickname is. . .
   a. Mr Muscles
   b. Fearless First Mate
   c. General Giggles
   d. Captain Tidypants

3. Francis's favourite animal is. . .
   a. duck-billed platypus
   b. koala
   c. cat
   d. gerbil

4. Francis has. . .

a. an aunt Patty

b. a baby sister

c. twin brothers

d. no siblings. He's an only child.

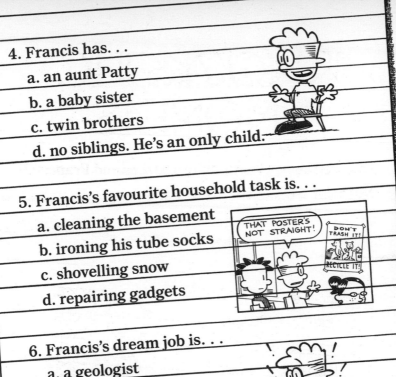

5. Francis's favourite household task is. . .

a. cleaning the basement

b. ironing his tube socks

c. shovelling snow

d. repairing gadgets

6. Francis's dream job is. . .

a. a geologist

b. an epidemiologist

c. a farmer

d. a professional wrestler

KNOCKOUT NOTES

Nate's notebook is filled with dramatic doodles! See if you can find all the things and people listed below and circle each one in Nate's notes on the opposite page.

BATHTUB

CLOWN

FRANKENSTEIN

SPITSY

PUPPET

BRICK WALL

LIGHTNING BOLT

KUNG FU MASTER

MAD SCIENTIST

RANDY

BASKETBALL

ULTRA-NATE

DUCK

SPACESHIP

CUBE

HEART

NOUGHTS AND CROSSES GAME

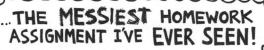

GUESS WHO?

How well do you know all the cool characters in Nate's world? Using the clues, see how fast you can solve this crossword puzzle!

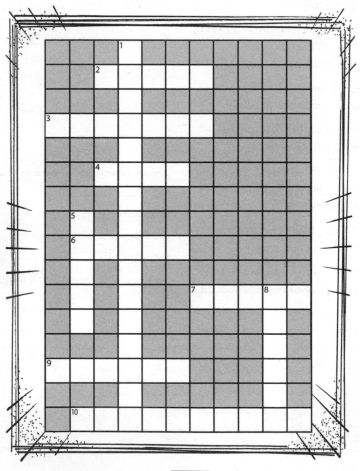

CLUES

ACROSS

2. Mr Perfect and Jenny's boyfriend.

3. Nate's #1 best friend; he LOVES trivia and colour coordinating his socks.

4. Know-it-all and teacher's pet, also Nate's enemy.

6. Nate's big sister (who's a little full of herself!)

7. Nate's other best friend; he's super-funny and awesome at sports.

9. He teaches art, Nate's favourite class!

10. Nate's social studies teacher, also known as Godzilla.

DOWN

1. He's the boss at P.S. 38 and runs the school.

5. She's so cute that Nate's had a crush on her since first grade.

8. She's one super drama queen!

SUPER SPY

Where should Dee Dee, super spy,
look for the missing camera?

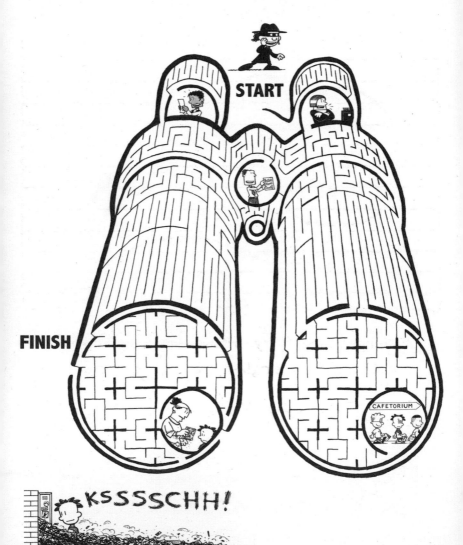

THE
SCRIBBLER

Play the scribble game!

Challenge yourself! Try writing a caption with your left hand if you're right-handed, or vice versa.

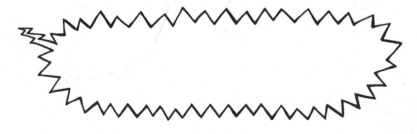

CANDID CAMERA

Gina, Nate's rival, wants to be yearbook editor. Why? So that she can feature great photos of. . . guess who? GINA!

WRITE A FUNNY CAPTION
FOR EACH PHOTO!

_____

_____

_____

_____

_____

_____

_____
_____
_____

_____
_____
_____
_____

_____
_____
_____

_____
_____
_____

GAG ME!

The kids at P.S. 38 love to trade totally gross Gag Me cards, even though they aren't allowed at school! Make the most disgusting Gag Me card characters by drawing lines from List A to List B!

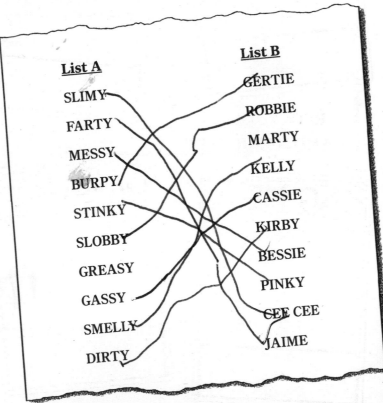

List A

SLIMY
FARTY
MESSY
BURPY
STINKY
SLOBBY
GREASY
GASSY
SMELLY
DIRTY

List B

GERTIE
ROBBIE
MARTY
KELLY
CASSIE
KIRBY
BESSIE
PINKY
CEE CEE
JAIME

DRAW YOUR OWN GAG ME CARDS WITH CHARACTERS AS YUCKY AS <u>SNOTTY SCOTTY</u>.

↰WRITE YOUR CARD NAME HERE.

THINKING CAPS

When Nate's trivia team compete, they put on their thinking caps. See if you can find all the caps listed below in the puzzle on the opposite page!

TIARA

SOMBRERO

BEANIE

SWIM CAP

BERET

BONNET

BASEBALL CAP

VISOR

BANDANNA

HELMET

FEDORA

BOWLER

FEZ

COWBOY HAT

TURBAN

TOP HAT

FASCINATOR

CROWN

```
S N R H N C B T E R E B S
T T V E O R O S I V A A R
A A H L B O T L E A T M D
S H W M O W A I T U R R F
E Y I E W N N R R P L A A
H O E T L A N B E C S O L
C B A S E B A L L C A P M
H W E B R N D O I A T A R
T O P H A T N N I W R C O
N C O Z O A A O L L A M R
R E E P O T B N B R H I O
A F E D O R A T M D E W S
O R E R B M O S A O S S C
```

BRAIN BOWL

Are you ready to test your brain big-time? Get ready for some totally tough trivia! Don't worry, you will surpass all others!

1. Which continent is the farthest north?

N̲ORth AmeriCa

2. What insect has eight legs?

S̲pider

3. Which planet is known for its rings?

S̲aturn

4. What does a caterpillar transform into?

B̲utterfly

5. Tokyo is the capital city of which country?

J a p a n

6. What organ pumps your blood?

H e a r t

7. What shape has three sides?

T r i a n g l e

8. What gas do we need to breathe to stay alive?

O x y g e n

9. What are the names of the five oceans on Earth?

A n t a r c t i c
P a c i f i c
I n d i a n
A r t i c
S o u t h e r n

10. Where can you find the Empire State Building?

N e w y o r k

FUNKY FITNESS

You may not think these activities are types of fitness. . . but they are! Can you fill out the grid so that each letter appears once in every row, every column, and every shaded box?

D = **DANCING**

M = **MALL WALKING**

C = **CURLING**

F = **FINGER JOUSTING**

D	M	C	
F		D	M
	D		C

NATE NERD

Are you an über-brain when it comes to Nate-tastic trivia? Let's see! Put that thinking cap to work, and circle either true or false for each statement.

---

1. Mrs Godfrey gave Nate an A++.

☐ TRUE   ☐ FALSE

---

2. Chad is afraid of cats.

☐ TRUE   ☐ FALSE

---

3. Teddy is the lead singer in Nate's band, Enslave the Mollusk.

☐ TRUE   ☐ FALSE

4. Principal Nichols asks Nate to be a hall monitor.

☐ TRUE   ☐ FALSE

5. Uncle Pedro is related to Artur.

☐ TRUE   ☐ FALSE

6. Francis has a job delivering newspapers.

☐ TRUE   ☐ FALSE

FACE-OFF!

Whoa! Check out these wacky faces from the candid photos in Nate's yearbook. See if you can draw the same face in the blank box next to each picture!

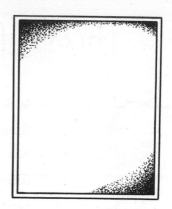

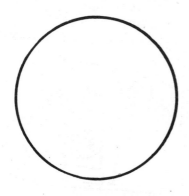

ROOM RAID

Take a look at Nate's bedroom – it's majorly messy! See if you can find all the items below and circle each one on the opposite page.

BANANA PEEL

SOCCER BALL

BASEBALL

BRUINS POSTER

PHOTO STRIP

BASEBALL CARD

RED SOX PENNANT

GOLF CLUBS

MONKEY STICKER

DOCTOR CESSPOOL COMIC

PORT CITY BIKES BUMPER STICKER

3 SOCKS

COMIX

SPIDER

PENCIL

DARTBOARD

SPIDER'S WEB

BASEBALL CAP

BOBCATS BAG

LAMP

MRS GODFREY DRAWING

SALTY SAM'S CRACKERS

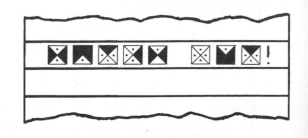

SCHOOL SCRAMBLE

Gina, the teacher's pet, sure loves school! What is Gina up to now? Draw a line from each school location to the correct photo below.

IT'S A
WONDERFUL LIFE

Why is Nate flipping out?

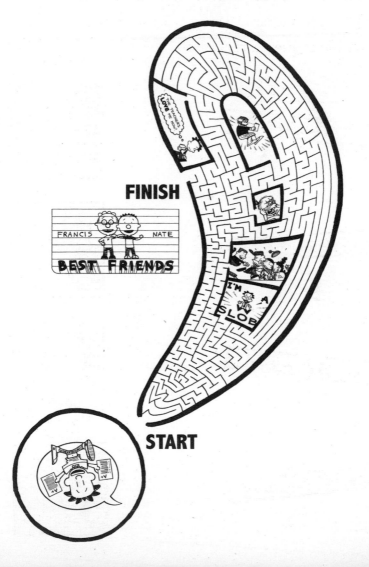

PASS THAT CLASS!

What's the subject of today's class? Big Nate, obviously! Get your pencils ready – you're sure to ace this one.

1. Mr Galvin was once part of this group.

a. Enslave the Mollusk

b. Mathletes

c. Timber Scouts

d. The P.S. 38 Jazzercise Team

2. Who is P.S. 38's most annoying hall monitor?

a. Dee Dee

b. Randy

c. Francis

d. Nick Blonsky

3. What is Teddy's uncle's name?

a. Uncle Francis

b. Uncle Pedro

c. Mr Holloway

d. Chad

4. Who likes to wear disguises?

a. Spitsy

b. Randy

c. Artur

d. Dee Dee

EXTRA CREDIT!
Who gets crazy about keeping
his lawn tidy?

a. Nate's dad

b. Mr McTeague

c. Mrs Godfrey

d. Francis

HERE, class! After you complete the FIRST sheet like GINA has, do this ridiculously confusing ADVANCED CALCULUS!

YAY!

What?

Still working on question #1

Chad→

READY, SET, CLICK

Nate wants to be a photographer for the yearbook – by taking lots of <u>crazy</u> candid photos! If you can find all the photo terms in this puzzle, you are a master behind the camera!

CANDID

CLOSE-UP

COMPOSITION

CAMERA

EXPOSURE

ANGLE

ZOOM

CROP

DARKROOM

SMILE

BACKLIGHTING

FLASH

FILM

NEGATIVES

PRINTS

SUBJECT

BULB

PHOTOGRAPHER

FOCUS

LENS

POSE

S	L	C	R	S	U	B	J	E	C	T	A
M	M	A	R	E	M	A	C	B	R	S	N
O	D	I	D	N	A	C	S	U	P	U	G
O	S	N	L	B	L	K	I	L	U	C	L
R	S	D	P	E	H	L	D	B	E	O	E
K	N	E	G	A	T	I	V	E	S	F	X
R	E	H	P	A	R	G	O	T	O	H	P
A	L	O	Z	P	R	H	S	A	L	F	O
D	R	O	P	L	A	T	F	P	C	M	S
C	O	M	P	O	S	I	T	I	O	N	U
M	T	C	P	R	I	N	T	S	L	S	R
R	I	A	D	H	S	G	R	P	U	M	E

MISERABLE MIDDLE NAMES

Nate's friend Francis gets teased because his middle name is Butthurst. Poor Francis! Draw lines from List A to List B below to create the <u>worst</u> middle names.

List A

BUTT

SLIME

FART

DIM

BURP

DORK

GROSS

SMELL

STINK

List B

SONG

MAN

KING

WIT

US

SON

ON

IT

FAST

NOW WRITE ALL THE MISERABLE MIDDLE NAMES YOU CREATED. RANK THEM FROM 1 (EMBARRASSING!) TO 10 (CAN'T EVER LIVE IT DOWN!!!).

NAME	RANK
1.	____
2. Dorkus	____
3.	____
4.	____
5.	____
6.	____
7. Burpsong	____
8.	____
9.	____
10.	____
11. Fartman	____
12.	____
13.	____
14.	____
15.	____

FRANCIS NEEDS TO GET **OVER** HIMSELF!

THERE ARE MIDDLE NAMES **WAY** WORSE THAN THAT!

FRANCIS
FACTOIDS

Can you fill in the grid so that each Francis fact only appears once in every row, column, and box?

C = **CAT PERSON**

T = **TRIVIA FANATIC**

S = **STUDYING MACHINE**

O = **ONLY CHILD**

N = **NEAT FREAK**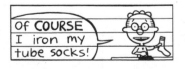

A = **AUNT PATTY CLONE!**

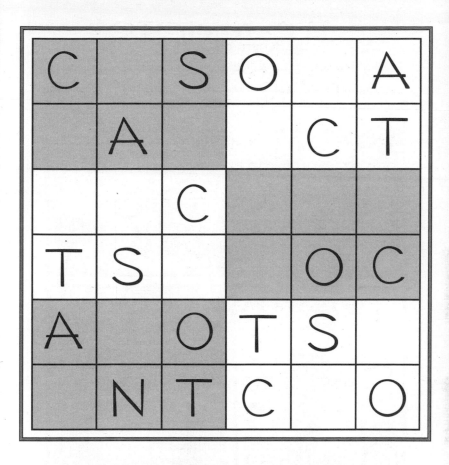

Chew at least **TWENTY TIMES** before swallowing!

And then **FLOSS** after eating!

* He doesn't have a moustache like Aunt Patty, but otherwise the similarities are **UNCANNY!**

PICTURE DAY

Uh-oh! It's the School Picture Guy – watch out!

Fill in the speech bubbles and decide what happens.

WHO'S WHO?

How well do you know all the kids at Nate's school?
Draw a line from each kid to the correct name!

ERIC FLEURY

MARY ELLEN POPOWSKI

RANDY BETANCOURT

TEDDY ORTIZ

DEE DEE HOLLOWAY

GINA HEMPHILL-TOMS

FRANCIS POPE

CHAD APPLEWHITE

GIRL WHO DRAWS UNICORNS

MASH-UP MAYHEM

**Quick! Make your own comic using
Coach John, a butterfly, and Dee Dee!**

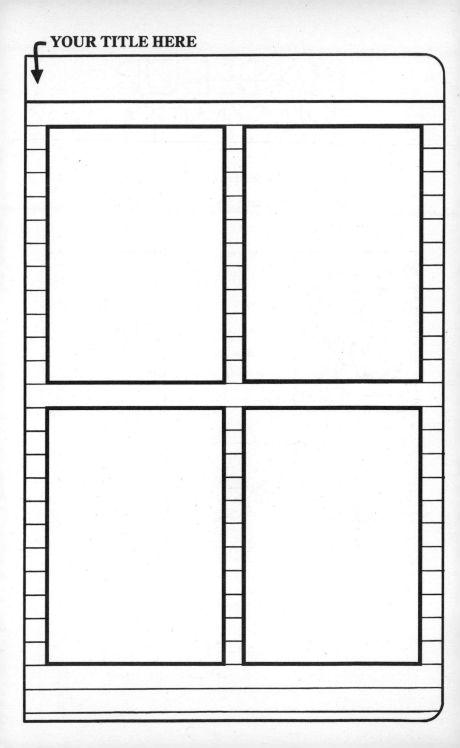

YOUR TITLE HERE

CHEEZ, PLEASE!

CRUNCH
CRUNCH

What's Nate's all-time favourite food? Scrumptious and delicious Cheez Doodles, of course! He's even written poems about them! See if you can solve the puzzle and find all the reasons Nate goes crazy for Cheez Doodles!

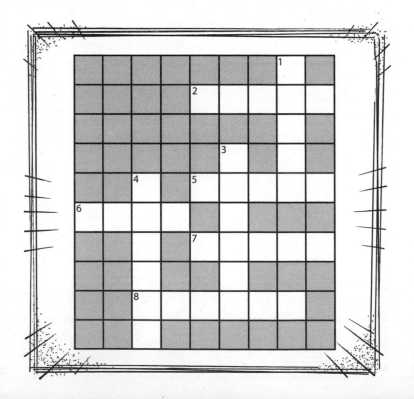

NATE! YOU **LOVE** CHEEZ DOODLES! YOU WRITE **POEMS** ABOUT THEM!

CLUES

ACROSS

2. This means delicious and rhymes with "tummy"!

5. Not baked but _____, this rhymes with "hide."

6. Rhymes with "girl." The shape of the Doodle.

7. Nate's favourite after-school _____ that keeps him satisfied until dinner!

8. Rhymes with "breezy." This is the flavor that makes them so irresistible!

DOWN

1. What Nate does when he eats them – the opposite of a frown!

3. Mix red and yellow together to make this color.

4. The sound of devouring a Doodle. It rhymes with "munch."

NOBODY CAN EAT CHEEZ DOODLES WITHOUT GETTING ALL POWDERY!

YEAH, THE POWDER IS WHAT MAKES 'EM SO **CHEESY-LICIOUS!**

WIPE
WIPE
WIPE
WIPE
WIPE
WIPE

MESS-O-METER

... BECAUSE YOU'RE SO **MESSY!**

Nate's notorious for being a mess – rank these from eww to gross out!

1. Spray cheese in your socks

☐ EWW   ☐ GAG ME

☐ YUCK   ☐ GROSS OUT

2. Bogeys on your desk

ANYBODY GOT A TISSUE?

☐ EWW   ☐ GAG ME

☐ YUCK   ☐ GROSS OUT

3. Mouldy tuna sandwich in your locker

☐ EWW   ☐ GAG ME

☐ YUCK   ☐ GROSS OUT

4. Spit in the corner of your teacher's mouth

☐ EWW   ☐ GAG ME

☐ YUCK   ☐ GROSS OUT

5. Flies land on your burger

☐ EWW ☐ GAG ME

☐ YUCK ☐ GROSS OUT

6. Stinky six-month-old gym shorts

☐ EWW ☐ GAG ME

☐ YUCK ☐ GROSS OUT

7. Slimy bologna from last week's lunch

☐ EWW ☐ GAG ME

☐ YUCK ☐ GROSS OUT

8. Grease all over your notebook

☐ EWW ☐ GAG ME

☐ YUCK ☐ GROSS OUT

HOUSE OF CARDS

Teddy's uncle Pedro uses playing cards to hypnotise Nate. What's in the cards for you? See if you can find each of these playing-card terms in the puzzle on the opposite page.

SPADE

QUEEN

DIAMOND

CLUB

JOKER

ACE

DECK

HAND

LUCKY

FLUSH

GAME

CARD

HEART

KING

JACK

FULL HOUSE

CHANCE

DEAL

```
K O N C Y J H B O K
C C L K C S O D E I
N E C L U B N K H N
F U L L H O U S E G
L K F H M H N N A R
D C H A N C E M R D
D E I J L A E I T N
E D A P S R U O H A
J C L L U D Q L E H
K I A N E N D U S K
```

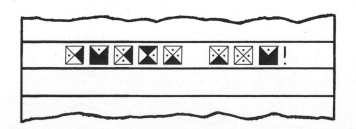

WHAP!! AWKWARD!

Nate and his friends always find themselves in sticky situations. List your TOP 20 most awkward moments!

1.

2.

3.

4.

5. Having toilet paper stuck to you

6.

7.

8. Throwing up in gym class

9.

10.

11.

12. Burping in maths class

13.

14.

15.

16.

17.

18. Getting tangled in a jump rope

19.

20.

GINA GALLERY

Yearbook editor, teacher's pet, Nate's nemesis! Can you capture the many faces of Gina? Copy each Gina face in one of the blank boxes below.

Help Nate's favourite private eye, Luke Warm, solve the case! Fill in the speech bubbles to finish the story!

GET SET, SCRIBBLE

**Can you play the scribble game
with your eyes <u>closed</u>?**

Open your eyes and write a caption.

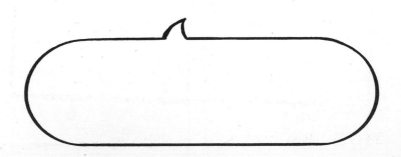

YOUR OWN YEARBOOK

What if there was a yearbook all about <u>you</u>? Obnoxious Gina would call hers The Ginacle.

NOW DESIGN YOUR OWN COVER!

TITLE: _____

HIDEAWAY!

Nate jams in the garage with his band, Enslave the Mollusk. Where do you and your friends hang out? See if you can hunt down all these hideaways in the puzzle!

CORNER STORE

GYM

MUSIC ROOM

GAZEBO

LIBRARY

TENT

GAME ROOM

COMIC BOOK STORE

TREE HOUSE

BASEMENT

BUNK BED

GARAGE

ATTIC

FORT

FOREST

```
N T O F M R M R C E F R T T
R I B E O O T F O M S C B E
B G A M E R O O M G R U O T
C T C O T B R R I R N E R M
O O Y O E H A T C K Y E A S
G B R Z E E O N B I E S F R
C A A N R C C E O H S O G R
T G R B E R D T O A R U Y E
E B B A S R R U K E E T M O
A T I A G O S E S R T C O N
U S L T G E A T T I C T M S
E R I R K I E C O N C I T T
O T O Y T R O N R R O I O I
B O R R R B A S E M E N T O
```

...BEANBAG CHAIRS!

FLUMP!

ZONED OUT

What happens when Nate's boring science teacher
is droning on? Or his sister is bragging again?
He spaces out!
LIST your TOP
15 zoned-out
moments!!

NOBODY LIKES
A SHOW-OFF, SON.
WHEN YOU CALL
ATTENTION TO YOUR-
SELF DURING
CLASS, IT REC
BLAH BLAH
BLAH BLAH
BLAH BLA
BLAH BLAH
BLAH

---

1. You've been playing your favourite video game
   for hours!

2.

3. You're staring at your crush of 5 years.

4.

5.

6.

7.

8. You're in class. It's snowing outside, and you're dreaming of snowboarding.

9.

GROAN

10.

11.

12.

13. You ate too many Cheez Doodles – MUST HAVE MORE! They've fried your brain.

14.

15.

ELLEN IS A **JOY** TO TEACH!

NEVER HAVE I HAD SUCH A DEDICATED STUDENT!

HER SUNNY DISPOSITION **LIGHTS UP** THE CLASSROOM!

SHE'S AN **INSPIRATION** TO **EVERYONE** AROUND HER!

1,2,3... SNAP!

Solve the maze and find
the funniest photo of all!

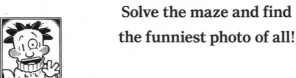

START

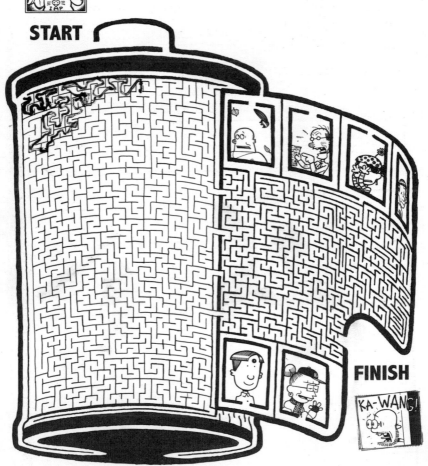

FINISH

BEST FRIENDS FOREVER

Me and Francis in kindergarten

Nate and Francis have been best friends since they were little – they even have a secret code! Who's <u>your</u> best friend?

ALL ABOUT MY BFF

BFF's name: _____

Nickname: _____

Favourite song: _____

Pet's name: _____

Favourite colour: _____

Hobby: _____

Best school subject: _____

Most loved food: _____

Favourite game ever: _____

NEAT FREAK

Nate's best friend Francis is so neat he colour-codes his underwear! What are your top 15 NEAT-FREAK moments? List them below, then rank them from 1 (tidy) to 10 (clean queen/king)!

NEAT-FREAK MOMENT	RANK
1.	____
2.	____
3.	____
4.	____
5. Dusting the closet	____
6.	____
7.	____
8. Alphabetising my toys	____

9. _____ _____

10. _____ _____

11. _____ _____

12. _____ _____

13. Cleaning the inside of my gym shoes _____

14. _____ _____

15. _____ _____

WELL, **EXCUUUSE** ME FOR NOT BEING AS ORGANISED AS **YOU**, FRANCIS!

WE CAN'T **ALL** HAVE COLOUR-CODED **UNDERWEAR!**

YANK!

ODD JOB-A-THON

Teddy's uncle Pedro has oodles of odd jobs. See if you can spot them in the puzzle on the opposite page. If you find all 11, you get a free palm reading!

ROOFER

LANDSCAPER

MUSICIAN

PALM READER

CARPENTER

SMALL-ENGINE REPAIRMAN

HYPNOTIST

HAIR DRESSER

KNIFE SHARPENER

YOGA INSTRUCTOR

LIVE-BAIT SALESMAN

```
N R I E N D A R I E Y I L I A Y C Y A S
A A C S S K K I R S E I T I C S O N A L
M U S I C I A N T C N R R R L G E C L L
S M A L L E N G I N E R E P A I R M A N
E R M S R R P S T F S P A I S H G N E S
L O E A R S R L O M E L N E N I D I A H
A H A A T N R O E A M S O C C S A M E P
S M Y V M I R S F R T U H N C N N S L T
T N O P R E S S E R D R I A H R A A E O
I A M T N T P A U N A T P P R N A R P U
A A E O N O D C F E S E I R E P P S N V
B E O P R E T N E P R A C R P H E G E E
E N I S R O I I S M E E E M I I D N E U
V R P R R N N R S A T S N P N R O E E N
I E R A E L A N O T R O R D I T C I E R
L A S N K R R R S S R I I E O S E A R D
```

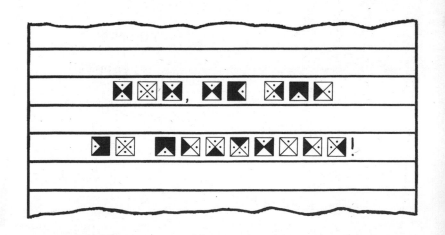

YEARBOOK LINE-UP

Take control of The Chronicle and become yearbook editor. Match each kid to the right title.

MOST AWESOME

SMARTEST

BIGGEST ATHLETE

MOST LIKELY TO SUCCEED

MOST THEATRICAL

BIGGEST BULLY

NICEST CLASSMATE

ACE PHOTOGRAPHER

Who takes the best photos at P.S. 38?

START

FINISH

REWARD ROUND UP

Nate's dad rewards him with a hot fudge sundae when he cleans his room. List your TOP 20 REWARDS ever!

1. A fluffy puppy!	16.
2.	17.
3.	18. a trip to the mall
4.	19.
5.	20.
6. jelly beans	
7.	
8.	
9.	
10.	
11.	
12.	
13.	
14.	
15.	

I THINK WE SHOULD MAKE SOME **HOT FUDGE SUNDAES!**

NOW DRAW THE MOST AWESOME REWARD YOU'VE EVER RECEIVED!

WACKY COMIX

What happens when you combine Dee Dee, Uncle Pedro, and Randy the bully? Watch out, big-time drama!

YOUR TITLE HERE

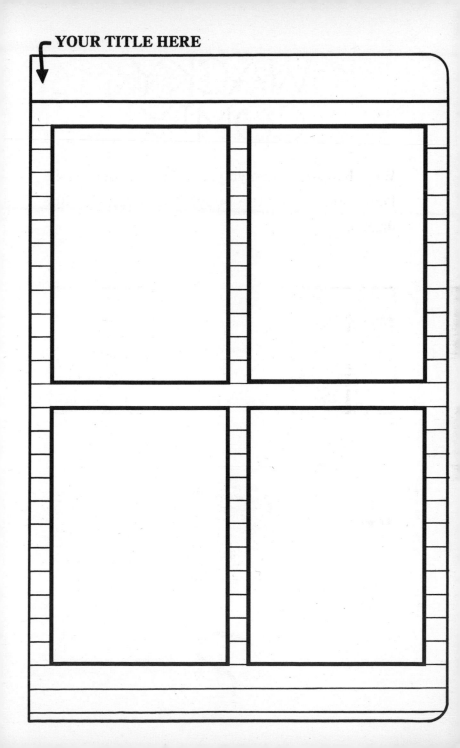

LUCKY CHARMS

Nate is superstitious. He believes in lucky charms. Fill in the grid so that each of these lucky charms shows up once in every row, column, and box!

P = **LUCKY PENNY**

R = **RABBIT'S FOOT**

F = **FOUR-LEAF CLOVER**

H = **HORSESHOE**

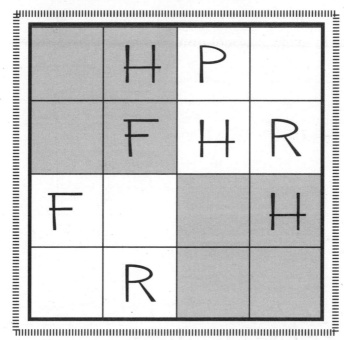

MEGA-MESS

Nate needs to clean up his act! Can you find all the messy and gross items in the puzzle on the opposite page?

BANANA PEEL

DEAD BUGS

CANDY WRAPPERS

PENCIL SHAVINGS

STINKY SOCKS

EGG SALAD SANDWICH

CHEESE

ROTTEN APPLE

KLEENEX

GYM SHORTS

HAIR GEL

OLD CHEWING GUM

OH. I... *KOFF!* ... I HAD A LITTLE ROOT BEER ACCIDENT.

HEH HEH!

S T R O H S M Y G M V D L R C A
T R X R A G I H E S H G E G S N
I Y E E D N R T G P D Y E H D G
N L N P I I C P Y S L H L S K A
K R E L P V U M D G I S S D A M
Y E E H H A I R G E L W A D M O
S U L R A H R S U K H N P E B L
O E K S E S S W T G N N S A B D
C H X H E L A T Y O D C N D I Y
K I C D N I P A D D H A E B A C
S P O L D C H E W I N G G U M H
H C I W D N A S D A L A S G G E
L R O T T E N A P P L E C S S E
E G E V P P S E E L N R Y S N S
N S V L S I E L D T C R T N S E
G B E C P L T E E C A K M D E A

YESTERDAY YOU WERE SUPPOSED TO SHARPEN YOUR PENCIL, NOT SPILL SHAVINGS ALL OVER THE FLOOR! SWEEP THAT UP!

TRIPLE-THREAT TEST

1. What is Francis's middle name?

a. Gross

b. Mudfart

c. Butthurst

d. Bogeyton

2. Which one of these characters is from Nate's comix?

a. Seymour Butts

b. Luke Warm

c. Harry Toes

d. Ivana Pea

3. Which trivia team is Randy on?

a. Francis's Factoids

b. Randy's Republic

c. Gina's Geniuses

d. Eric Fleury's Eggheads

4. What's Chad's superhero name?

a. Champion Chad

b. Chadtastic

c. Charming Chad

d. Mega-Chad

5. What is Dee Dee's last name?

a. Popowski

b. Pierce

c. Applewhite

d. Holloway

6. What kind of pet does Chad have?

a. Kuddle Kitten

b. gerbil

c. parakeet

d. turtle

NUTTY NICKNAMES

One of Nate's favourite hobbies is coming up with gross nicknames for his social studies teacher, Godzilla, aka Mrs Godfrey. Match the words below to make more nicknames for Nate's list!

NUTTER	PARADE
CRAZY	STINKER
DEATH	GARGOYLE
SASSY	BUTT
MEAN	BREATH
LADY	DRAGON
MEGA	QUEEN
GREASY	BUTTER
CUCKOO	PANTS
DOOM	DUCHESS

WRITE YOUR TOP 10 NICKNAMES HERE.

1.
2.
3.
4.
5.
6.
7.
8.
9.
10.

CRAZY CHARACTERS

Put on your thinking cap and make new character names for each person or animal below! The crazier, the better!

BULLY, BEWARE!

What's Randy the bully up to now? Fill in the speech bubbles and help Nate save the day!

DRAW YOURSELF HERE!!!

LAUGH ATTACK

Teddy is the ultimate jokester. Use the code on page 9 to find out the punch lines!

Q: What has one head, one foot, and four legs?

A:

_ _ _ _

Q: What sound do porcupines make when they kiss?

A: !

_ _ _ _!

HEH MMPH!
HEH! *SNORT!*

Q: What goes through towns and up hills but doesn't move?

A: !

_ _ _ _ _ _ _!

GROUCHY GODFREY

Geez, Nate's least favourite teacher, Mrs Godfrey, is ALWAYS grumpy! What's she growling about now? You decide. Fill in the bubbles!

QUICK DRAW!

Think fast! Draw a comic that includes
a pirate, Dee Dee, and Nate!

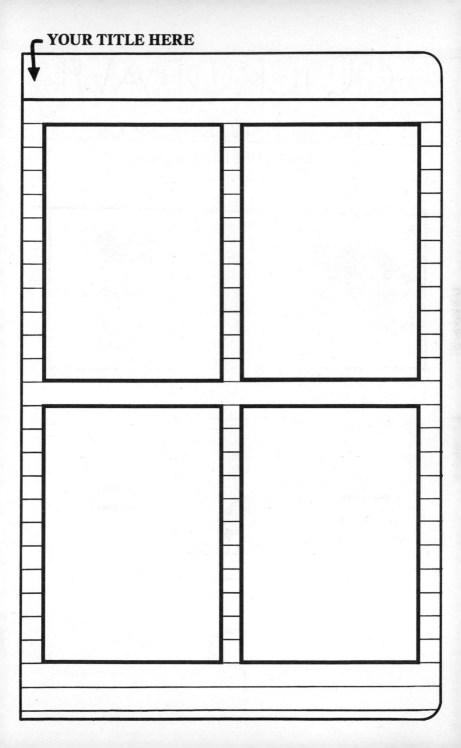

YOUR TITLE HERE

UNDERCOVER

Do you want to be an international spy or master of disguise, like Dee Dee? Draw lines from Column A to Column B below to create super-spy names!

Column A	Column B
DANGER	INVISIBLE
CAPTAIN	FLASH
SPEEDY	RANGER
DARK	AWESOME
SUPER	SQUIRREL
FLYING	SPARROW
SILVER	SENSATION
QUEEN	MYSTERY
MASTER	FLY
AMAZING	DYNAMO
SERGEANT	BOLT

WRITE YOUR TOP 10
SUPER-SPY NAMES HERE.

1.
2.
3.
4.
5.
6.
7.
8.
9.
10.

CAPTION
ACTION

You've been made yearbook editor of P.S. 38! Come up with funny captions for each photo and fill in the blanks!

_____

_____

_____

_____

_____

_____

_____

_____

_____

_____
_____
_____

_____
_____
_____

_____
_____
_____

_____
_____
_____

DARE TO DREAM

When you go to sleep, do you have outrageously crazy dreams, like Nate? List the TOP 20 wildest things you dream about! Then rank them from 1 to 20.

DREAM	RANK
1. Starring in a movie	_____
2.	_____
3.	_____
4. Fighting aliens	_____
5.	_____
6.	_____
7.	_____
8. Becoming a superhero	_____

YEEP!

9. Throwing slime on the school bully _____

10. _____

11. Riding a dinosaur _____

12. _____

13. _____

14. Winning the _____
    Trivia Slam

15. _____

16. _____

17. Swimming in marshmallows _____

18. _____

19. Getting your own reality TV show _____

20. _____

SECRET CRUSH

Nate's always had a HUGE crush on his classmate Jenny!
Now you play matchmaker. Draw lines from Column A
to Column B and decide who makes the cutest couples.

COLUMN A

COLUMN B

PRIVATE EYE

Luke Warm is about to crack the case of the missing camera. Fill in the speech bubbles and solve the crime!

SCHOOL YARD
COOL

Dee Dee loves to jump rope, and Teddy's the kickball king. What's at the top of your recess list? See if you can find all these awesome activities in the super search on the next page!

TETHERBALL

HOPSCOTCH

WALL BALL

LEAPFROG

HIDE-AND-SEEK

MONKEY BARS

TYRE SWING

FREEZE TAG

SLIDE

JUNGLE GYM

SOCCER

FOUR SQUARE

PARACHUTE

KICKBALL

```
E  Q  Z  E  N  Q  H  O  P  S  C  O  T  C  H
F  O  U  R  S  Q  U  A  R  E  I  T  Q  I  V
O  S  H  I  D  E  A  N  D  S  E  E  K  Z  K
P  H  N  D  K  X  T  L  S  Q  V  T  Q  U  I
M  A  Z  Q  F  V  Q  Y  A  L  Q  H  U  F  C
O  V  R  L  L  R  J  Q  R  Q  I  W  W  A  K
N  W  P  A  E  V  E  U  Y  E  Q  D  K  I  B
K  Y  A  F  C  A  D  E  N  Q  S  N  E  C  A
E  Z  R  L  O  H  P  Z  Z  G  H  W  C  Q  L
Y  F  Q  K  L  U  U  F  L  E  L  L  I  O  L
B  R  F  D  M  B  C  T  R  S  T  E  B  N  O
A  M  R  Z  X  H  A  E  E  O  Z  A  G  D  G
R  S  O  C  C  E  R  L  F  Q  G  A  G  Y  U
S  R  Q  W  V  H  W  L  L  C  I  I  K  O  M
R  O  Q  T  E  T  H  E  R  B  A  L  L  C  A
```

GINA! WANT TO JUMP ROPE IN THE SCHOOL YARD?

OK!

!

GINA
THE GREAT

Gina knows just how to annoy Nate BIG-time! How well do you know Gina? See if you can ace this quiz! True or false?

1. Gina plays drums in Nate's band.

☑ TRUE   ☐ FALSE

2. Nate's had a crush on Gina since first grade.

WHA-?

☐ TRUE   ☑ FALSE

3. Gina's the editor of the yearbook.

HERE'S WHAT I'VE DONE!

☑ TRUE   ☐ FALSE

4. Gina named Nate's fleeceball team the Kuddle Kittens.

STRIKE ONE!

☑ TRUE   ☐ FALSE

5. Mrs Godfrey is Gina's favourite teacher.

☑ TRUE   ☐ FALSE

6. Artur is dating Gina.

☐ TRUE   ☑ FALSE

GAWK!

BUBBLE TROUBLE

What is each character saying?? Fill in the speech bubbles as FAST as you can and create the fun!

SPLURCH!

NATE FACE-OFF!

Can you copy Nate's many faces? Go for it!

WHOSE LOCKER IS IT?

Nate is known for being SUPER messy, and his best friend Francis is a total neat freak. Which locker item is Nate's and which one belongs to Francis?

COLUMN A

SWEATY SOCKS

APPLE

TRIVIA BOOK

CHEEZ DOODLES

GROSS GYM SHORTS

TOOTHBRUSH

MR GALVIN'S DENTURES

MATHS HOMEWORK

CALCULATOR

MOULDY MOUTHGUARD

HEAD OF A LAWN GNOME

NAPKINS

SUNSCREEN

OLD TURKEY SANDWICH

COLUMN B

NATE

FRANCIS

NATE-TASTIC TRIVIA

OH! THAT REMINDS ME!...

Quick! Find out if you're the master of Nate-knowledge! Circle the right answer.

I CAN'T BELIEVE IT!

1. When Nate is hypnotised, how does he change?

YOU'RE LIKE A DIFFERENT PERSON!

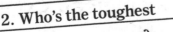

a. He starts wearing superhero costumes.

b. He becomes neat.

c. He becomes yearbook editor.

d. He dates Jenny (finally!).

2. Who's the toughest hall monitor ever?

IT'S SO OBVIOUS!

a. Gina Hemphill-Toms

b. Nick Blonsky

c. Francis

d. Randy Betancourt

3. What is the middle name of Nate's dramatic
   friend, Dee Dee?

   a. Butthurst
   b. Mud
   c. Dorcas
   d. Speaker

4. Who hypnotised Nate?

   a. Mrs Godfrey
   b. Gina
   c. Uncle Pedro
   d. Jenny

5. Nate's favourite sport is. . .

   a. basketball
   b. Jazzercise
   c. hockey
   d. fleeceball

STOP, DROP, AND DRAW!

Ready? Pick up that pencil!! Create a super-cool comic using these characters.

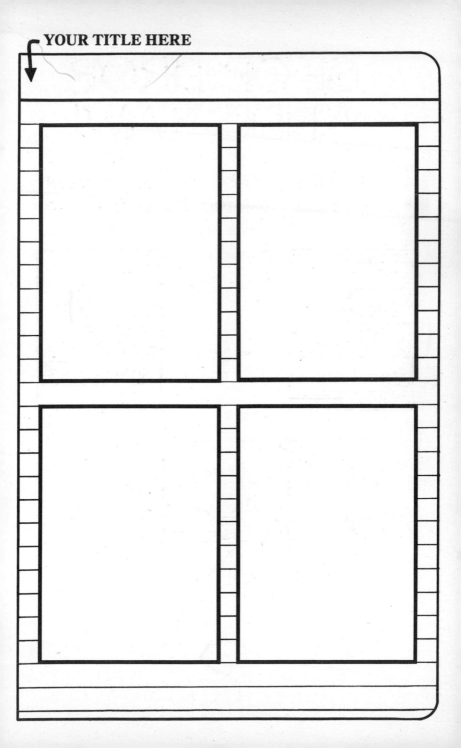

YOUR TITLE HERE

DETECTIVE DEE DEE

Dee Dee LOVES to solve school mysteries at P.S. 38! See if you can become a super sleuth too. Find all 15 words hidden in the puzzle!

SPY

SCENE

PRIVATE EYE

MYSTERY

HIDDEN

SPECIAL AGENT

EVIDENCE

SUSPECT

MAGNIFYING GLASS

INVESTIGATE

CRIME

SECRET

TRANCE

POLICE

CASE

E	I	T	N	Y	U	I	P	N	S	P	S	E	C	C
C	I	N	S	I	T	S	T	D	E	S	A	N	S	A
C	T	E	V	I	D	E	N	C	E	E	S	N	I	V
C	V	G	C	E	D	Y	E	G	G	L	C	F	R	N
S	D	A	D	W	S	N	D	S	D	C	S	L	T	N
U	E	L	O	N	S	T	D	G	I	R	Y	I	R	T
S	S	A	L	G	G	N	I	Y	F	I	N	G	A	M
P	M	I	O	P	P	N	H	G	R	M	C	G	N	E
E	T	C	I	O	Y	R	O	A	A	E	N	E	C	M
C	S	E	I	L	T	A	C	E	N	T	T	S	E	G
T	A	P	R	I	V	A	T	E	E	Y	E	S	S	P
A	Y	S	Y	C	G	I	C	O	C	Y	P	L	Y	P
S	V	E	E	E	E	S	M	E	I	R	D	Y	I	M
E	A	E	E	C	S	S	C	I	S	E	E	S	H	R
N	A	S	A	S	Y	I	A	T	C	F	Y	E	E	T

YES! AND I SAW HIM SHOWING SOMETHING TO HIS GANG! SOMETHING HE DIDN'T WANT ANYONE ELSE TO **SEE!**

WHISPER!
WHISPER!
HEH HEH!
HA HA!

RANDY ON THE RUN

Randy the bully is up to no good! Fill in the speech bubbles and decide what happens next!

SCRIBBLE
STATION

What will you turn your scribble into?

Don't forget to write a caption:

Fish

SNACK-TASTIC!

Chad goes mad for doughnuts, Nate is crazy for Cheez Doodles, and Dee Dee loves cinnamon buns. What about you? Rank these snacks from 1 to 10. 1 is just yum, and 10 is TOTALLY DELICIOUS!

SNACK	RANK
1. Gummy bears	_____
2. Chocolate-chip cookies	_____
3. Jelly beans	_____
4. Mixed nuts	_____
5. Crackers	_____
6. String cheese	_____
7. Apples and peanut butter	_____
8. Raisins	_____

9. Yogurt   ____

10. Granola bar   ____

11. Popcorn   ____

12. Pretzels   ____

13. Baby carrots   ____

14. Cheez Doodles   ____

15. Banana   ____

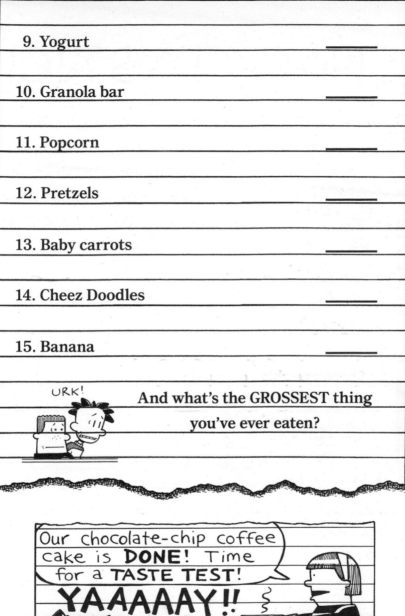

And what's the GROSSEST thing
you've ever eaten?

COPY SHOP

Quick! Put your cartooning skills to the test! Try drawing each of these characters in the blank boxes below.

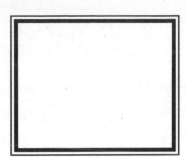

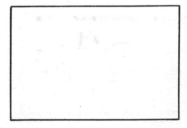

DAD DRAMA

Nate is one troublemaker who definitely drives his dad crazy! What do you do that makes your dad insane?

LIST YOUR TOP 20 HERE!

1.

2. Skateboarding in the dining room

3.

4.

5.

6.

7.

8. Picking your nose

9.

10.

11. Eating only potato chips for dinner

12.

13.

NATE... IS THERE ANYTHING YOU WANT TO TELL ME?

14. Dressing up the neighbour's cat

15.

16.

KA-WANG!

17. Putting worms in your sister's hair

18.

19. Leaving dirty socks everywhere

20.

⊠ ⊠ ⊠ ◣ ▶ !

Watch out, Nate's in trouble big-time. Fill in the speech bubbles and decide what they're yelling about! Then give each comic a crazy title.

WRITE YOUR TITLE HERE!

ROCKIN' OUT

Nate, Teddy, Artur, and Francis have their own band – Enslave the Mollusk!

What's your favourite band or pop star?

Name their best song:

What does the band wear onstage?

Name the #1 reason they're awesome!

NOW DRAW YOUR BAND PERFORMING FOR A HUGE CROWD!

DANCE FEVER

Can you bust a move like Nate and Dee Dee? See if you can find all the different dances in this hidden-word puzzle. Then join the dance party!

POLKA

HIP-HOP

BALLET

BREAK DANCE

HOKEY POKEY

TAP

SWING

FLAMENCO

MODERN

BELLY DANCE

JAZZ

SALSA

TANGO

DISCO

BALLROOM

WALTZ

HULA

TWIST

```
S A N C K O R B E A A
E L M L I Y G N I W S
A C O C N E M A L F L
E C N A D K A E R B A
D T R A P O L K A N S
I W E N D P G L Z H W
S I D O A Y L N I N A
C S O T H E L P A L L
O T M U T K H L A T T
B A L L R O O M E K Z
J A Z Z P H K G P B O
```

DANCE, BABY, DANCE!
SHAKESHAKESHAKE YOUR PANTS!
CLONK!   *SIGH.*   DOOF!

TALENT TIME

Nate's friend Teddy has a special trick – he can make fart noises with his armpit! What other weird talents do you think the kids at P.S. 38 have? Write them down next to each name!

Nate: _____

Chester: Blows yogurt out his nose _____

Dee Dee: _____

Gina: _____

Francis: _____

Teddy: Armpit fart _____

Jenny: _____

Artur: _____

Chad: _____

NAME YOUR TALENT! ↘

You: make singers be nice

REALLY? AWESOME!

EDITOR-IN-CHIEF

Who should be the editor of the Chronicle?

HOOP IT UP!

Nate's got some skills on the basketball court. Check out his jump shot! Let's see what you can do. Using the letters in "basketball," see how many words you can create!

BASKETBALL

1.
2.
3.
4.
5.
6.
7.
8.
9.
10.
11.
12.
13.
14.

15.

16.

17.

18.

19.

20.

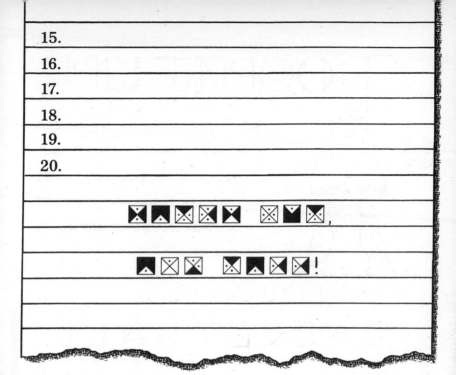

DRAMATIC FLASHBACK!

What happened before?
It's up to you! Draw it.

HOW DID NATE MAKE THIS MESS?

THEY'RE STICKING TO MY **HANDS!**

WHO HIT PRINCIPAL NICHOLS?

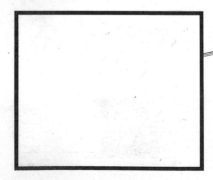

KLANG!

UH-OH! WHAT DID NATE DO NOW?

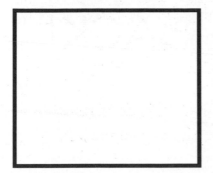

WHAT IS DEE DEE UP TO?

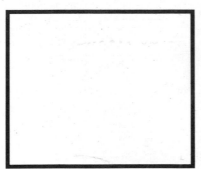

WHO THREW THE BOTTLE?

ANGER DANGER

Nate's up to his old tricks! How mad are his teachers now? Draw a line from each teacher to the right level on the rage meter.

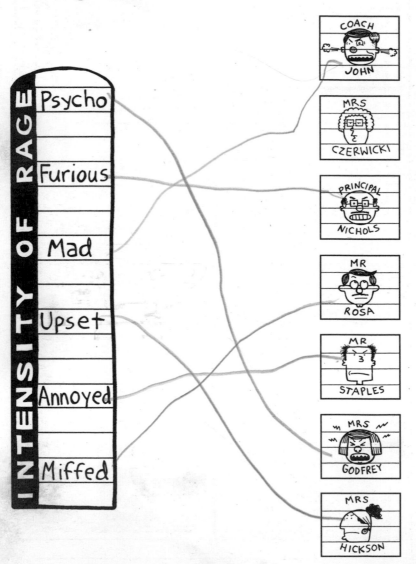

ULTRA-NATE AND MEGA-CHAD

These two are the ultimate team of superheroes!
Fill in the speech bubbles and help them save Maya!

LUCKY CHARMS

Chad has a special plastic foot that he carries with him for good luck. What's your lucky charm? Draw it!

NOW UNSCRAMBLE THE WORDS BELOW TO FIND MORE GOOD-LUCK CHARMS!

VRECLO _ _ _ _ _ _

(Clue: green; picked by leprechauns)

ARBBTI _ _ _ _ _ _

IT'S PART OF SOME SORT OF *ACTION FIGURE!*

TOFO _ _ _ _

(Clue: bunny paw)

OSRHESOHE _ _ _ _ _ _ _ _ _

(Clue: bigger than a pony; footwear)

RSAT _ _ _ _

(Clue: Shines brightly!)

RIGHT AFTER YOU LEFT FOR THE PRINCIPAL'S OFFICE, I FOUND IT ON THE FLOOR OF THE CAFETORIUM!

AIBROWN _ _ _ _ _ _ _

(Clue: There's a pot of gold at the end!)

BOOK NOOK

Nate spends a lot of time in the library, even though the librarian, Mrs Hickson, is not his biggest fan! What about you?

QUICK QUIZ:

1. What is your favourite book?

2. Who's the character that you like best?

3. If you gave the book a new title, what would it be?

4. If you could create a new cover for the book, what would it look like?

DRAW IT HERE.

DOODLEMANIA!

Nate fills his whole notebook with doodles – how about you? We dare you!

MR PERFECT

Annoyingly perfect Artur has joined Nate's band! What will happen next? Fill in the speech bubbles, and fast!

LOVE FEST

Teddy loves sports,
Nate loves comix,
and Artur loves Jenny!

WHICH OF THESE THINGS DO YOU LOVE MOST? RATE THEM FROM 1 (HO-HUM) TO 10 (INFATUATION).

	RATING
· Pizza party	_____
· Playing with your pet	_____
· Ice-cream sundaes	_____
· Ping Pong	_____
· Amusement park	_____
· Skateboarding	_____
· Board games	_____
· Jelly beans	_____

ROWR! HEE HEE!
WOOF!
WORF!

- Trick-or-treating   _____

- Pyjama Day at school   _____

- Camping   _____

- Flying a kite   _____

- Building a sand castle   _____

- Jumping on your bed   _____

- Visiting your grandparent   _____

- Playing baseball   _____

- Dancing   _____

- Peanut butter and jelly sandwiches   _____

- Swimming in the ocean   _____

- Climbing a tree   _____

COMIX
CAPTAIN

Create your own comic using Chad,
a sabre-toothed swamp cat, and Coach John!

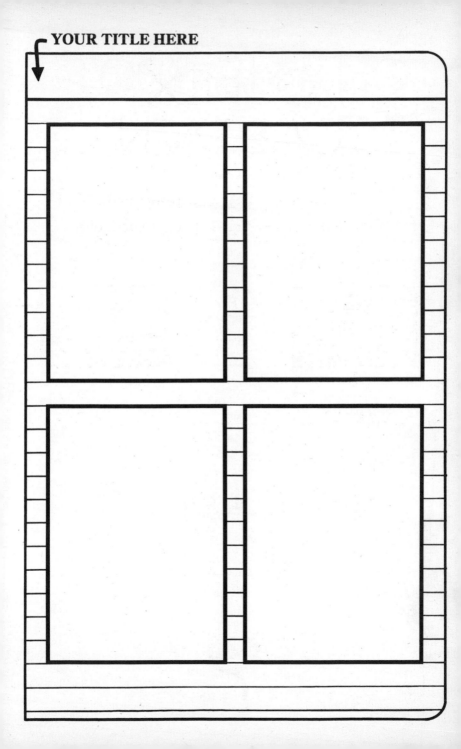

YOUR TITLE HERE

ON THE SPOT

Are you the master of Nate knowledge?
Prove it! Do you think these statements
are true or false?

1. Nate loves Jazzercise.

☐ TRUE   ☑ FALSE

2. Stuffed cabbage is Chad's favourite meal.

☐ TRUE   ☑ FALSE

3. Mrs Godfrey is Nate's favourite teacher.

☐ TRUE   ☑ FALSE

4. Chad likes Maya.

☑ TRUE   ☐ FALSE

5. Artur is the lead singer in Nate's band.

☑ TRUE   ☐ FALSE

6. Dee Dee is really shy.

☐ TRUE   ☑ FALSE

7. Chad's lucky charm is a plastic foot.

☐ TRUE   ☑ FALSE

8. Nate's dad is dating Mrs Godfrey.

☐ TRUE   ☑ FALSE

9. Francis plays the guitar.

☐ TRUE   ☑ FALSE

10. Teddy's uncle hypnotises people.

☐ TRUE   ☑ FALSE

11. Gina is Nate's best friend.

WHA-?...
SPUTTER!

☐ TRUE   ☑ FALSE

MMM, GOOD!

MMMMMM!

SNIFF
SNIFF
SNUFF
SNUFF

Chad loves the smell of Ms Brindle's class because it always smells like cinnamon!

NAME YOUR TOP 15 BEST SMELLS EVER:

1.

2.

3.

4. blueberry pancakes

5.

6.

7. chocolate cupcakes

8.

9. roses

10.

11.

...GOOD!

12.

13.

14.

15.

MORNING MADNESS

Oh no, Claude, the stupid ideas fairy, visited Teddy for breakfast! Is disaster about to happen? You decide.

FAST-FORWARD

Can you tell the future? You decide what happens after each scene, then draw it!

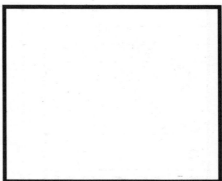

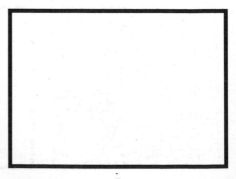

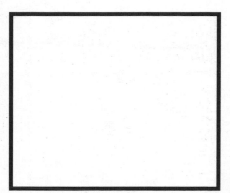

MASTERMIND

Pop quiz time! Don't sweat it – you've got this. Test your Nate trivia now!

1. Chad is covered in. . .

   a. sprinkles

   b. chicken pox

   c. beanbag pellets

   d. dirt

2. The nicest teacher at P.S. 38 is. . .

   a. Mrs Godfrey

   b. Mr Staples

   c. Coach John

   d. Mr Rosa

3. Nate's two best friends are. . .

a. Randy and Marcus

b. Francis and Teddy

c. Maya and Dee Dee

d. Spitsy and Pickles

4. Who's the biggest bully?

a. Mr Galvin

b. Randy

c. Marcus

d. Pickles

HYPNOSIS CENTRAL

Where should Nate go to get hypnotised?

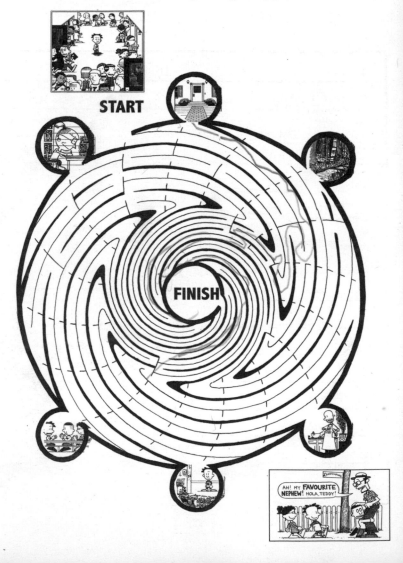

DETENTION PREVENTION

Principal Nichols has CANCELLED Nate's detention!

List all the fun things Nate's going to do now!

1.	16.
2. Eat cookies	17.
3.	18. Walk Spitsy
4.	19.
5.	20.
6. Play fleeceball	
7.	
8.	
9.	...I'LL HAVE TO **CANCEL** YOUR **DETENTION!**
10.	
11.	
12.	
13. Tease Gina	
14.	
15.	

BAND AID

Help Nate's band write some new songs for
their next show! Fill in the blanks!

We're here to _____ ,

It's time to _____ ,

The beat is _____ on _____ ,

Just hear our _____ ,

The crowd goes _____ ,

For you, _____ child _____ ,

Hey, P.S. _____thirty-eight_____,

You know you're _____,

Just like _____,

'Cause he's our _____,

He's super _____fly_____,

Oh yeah, we _____,

We're here to _____!

HERE NOW, TO TELL YOU ALL ABOUT IT IN AN ORIGINAL SONG, IS P.S. 38's VERY OWN...

ENSLAVE THE MOLLUSK!

YAAAAY!

COMIX BY U!

Get ready! Create a comic using Principal Nichols, Nate, and a plastic bottle. I smell trouble!

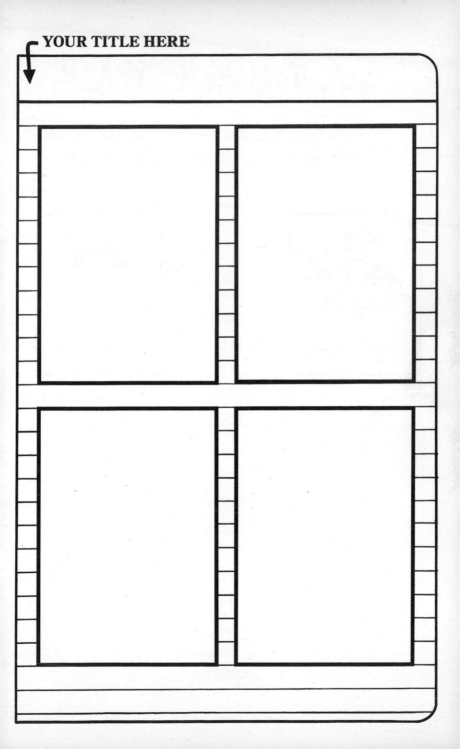

YOUR TITLE HERE

WOW WORDS

Nate has one very cool spot in the library – the beanbag chairs! Using the letters in the words "beanbag chair," see if you can make more than 20 other words!

BEANBAG CHAIR

1.	12.
2.	13.
3.	14.
4.	15.
5.	16.
6.	17.
7.	18.
8.	19.
9.	20.
10.	21.
11.	22.

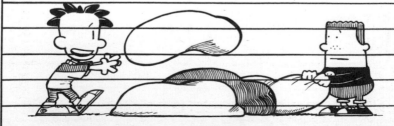

MUSIC MAN

Chad plays oboe in the school band at P.S. 38.

DO YOU PLAY AN INSTRUMENT? WHICH ONE?

DRAW IT HERE!

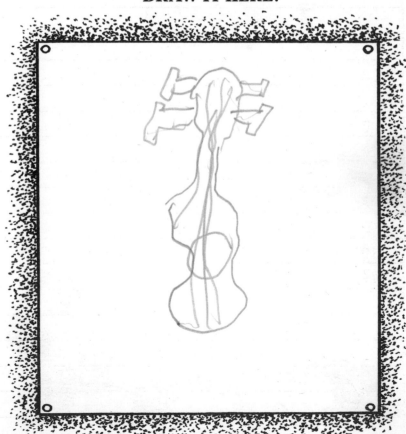

NOW SEE IF YOU CAN FIND ALL THE DIFFERENT INSTRUMENTS IN THIS HIDDEN-WORD PUZZLE!

DRUM

TROMBONE

HARP

CLARINET

FLUTE

GUITAR

SAXOPHONE

PICCOLO

TRIANGLE

CYMBALS

VIOLA

TRUMPET

TUBA

FRENCH HORN

PIANO

OBOE

VIOLIN

BASS

```
T C T E P M U R T H L M
O A I N N G R P U C M N
N I L O I V I P O U G N
N R O H H C N E R F I B
M P B P C A O D O T Y F
L T R O M B O N E B I L
I A L X G P O N L P O U
H O S A S U I O E A A T
C I A S T R I A N G L E
C Y M B A L S T N F O N
C A G L U B T O A O I N
I A C I B T C A L R V L
```

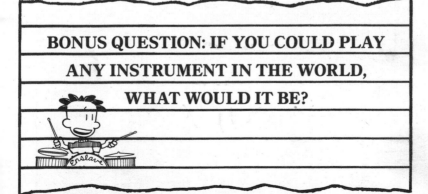

BONUS QUESTION: IF YOU COULD PLAY ANY INSTRUMENT IN THE WORLD, WHAT WOULD IT BE?

GAME ON!

Nate and Chad are in the middle of a heated hockey game in gym class. Using the letters in the words "hockey stick," see if you can create more than 20 other words and help Nate win the game!

HOCKEY STICK

1.	15.
2.	16.
3.	17.
4. yoke	18.
5.	19. key
6.	20.
7.	21.
8.	22.
9.	
10.	
11.	
12.	
13. kick	
14.	

ARE YOU A HOCKEY CHAMP, LIKE NATE?

☐ YES   ☐ NO

LET'S SEE YOUR SKILLS!
DRAW A PICTURE OF YOURSELF
PLAYING HOCKEY HERE!

COMIX
CONNECTION

It's time for an awesome comix connection!
Draw a comic using Chad and Maya –
show how they first meet!

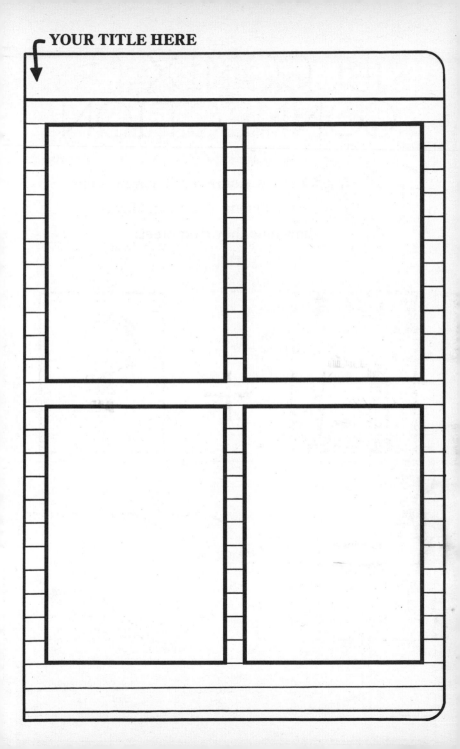

YOUR TITLE HERE

SIBLING RIVALRY

Me and Ellen

Do you have a brother or sister?
Nate's older sister, Ellen, can be
a serious pain sometimes!

LIST THE TOP 10 THINGS
YOUR BROTHER OR SISTER
DOES THAT ANNOY YOU.

1. cracks butts and coconuts
2. No sense of humor
3. Eats all the cereal.
4.
5.
6.
7.
8. Uses my stuff without asking!
9.
10.

NOW, WHAT ARE THE TOP 10 THINGS
YOU LOVE ABOUT YOUR BROTHER
OR SISTER?

1.
2.
3.
4.
5.
6.
7.
8.
9.
10.

DRAW A PICTURE OF YOU
WITH YOUR SIBLINGS!

FUNNY BONE

Teddy is one funny jokester! Using his secret code below, figure out the punch lines to Teddy's seriously silly jokes.

A	B	C	D	E	F	G	H	I	J	K	L	M
Z	Y	X	W	V	U	T	S	R	Q	P	O	N

N	O	P	Q	R	S	T	U	V	W	X	Y	Z
M	L	K	J	I	H	G	F	E	D	C	B	A

Q: Why did the picture go to jail?

A: $\overline{Y}\ \overline{V}\ \overline{X}\ \overline{Z}\ \overline{F}\ \overline{H}\ \overline{V}\quad \overline{R}\ \overline{G}$

$\overline{D}\ \overline{Z}\ \overline{H}\quad \overline{U}\ \overline{I}\ \overline{Z}\ \overline{N}\ \overline{V}\ \overline{W}$.

Q: What did the paper say to the pencil?

A: $\overline{}\ \overline{}\ \overline{}\ \overline{}\ \overline{}\ \overline{}\ \overline{}$!

D I R G V L M

Q: Why was the broom late?

A: $\overline{}\ \overline{}\ \overline{}\ \overline{}\ \overline{}\ \overline{}\ \overline{}\ \overline{}\ \overline{}\ \overline{}\ \overline{}$!

R G L E V I H D V K G

Q: What goes up and down but does not move?

A: $\overline{}\ \overline{}\ \overline{}\ \overline{}\ \overline{}\ \overline{}$.

H G Z R I H

Q: How do you make a walnut laugh?

A: $\overline{}\ \overline{}\ \overline{}\ \overline{}\ \overline{}\ \overline{}\ \overline{}\ \overline{}\ \overline{}$!

X I Z X P R G F K

GODZILLA

Who's Nate's scariest teacher, nicknamed Godzilla?
Mrs Godfrey! For each letter in her name, write down
an adjective or phrase that describes her, beginning
with that letter. Do it before you get detention!

M_____

R_____

S cary_____

G_____

O_____

D_____

F_____

R_____

E_____

Y_____

MEGA-CHAD THE MARVEL

Did you think that Nate's friend Chad was shy? Well, he might surprise you! He's a student by day, superhero by night. Fill in the speech bubbles and finish the adventure!

STAGE FRIGHT

DURING MY THIRD-GRADE PRODUCTION OF "ALICE IN WONDERLAND," I FORGOT **ALL MY LINES!**

I JUST **STOOD** THERE SAYING **NOTHING!**

When Dee Dee was in "Alice in Wonderland," she forgot her lines and just stood there saying NOTHING!

LIST YOUR TOP 10 STAGE FRIGHT FREAK-OUTS.

1.
2.
3.
4.
5.
6.
7. There was toilet paper stuck to my costume!
8.
9.
10.

STAR POWER

Will Enslave the Mollusk become the next big boy band and top the charts? You decide – fill out the speech bubbles and make Nate famous!

SCHOOL STORY

Nate's school, P.S. 38, is pretty cool – the mascot is the Bobcat; there's the Doodlers, their cartooning club; and they play fleeceball!

What's your school story?

YOUR SCHOOL NAME:

_____

MASCOT:

_____

SCHOOL COLOURS:

_____

CLUBS YOU BELONG TO:

_____

FAVOURITE TEACHER:

_____

MOST EXCITING AFTER-SCHOOL EVENT:

_____

BIGGEST RIVAL SCHOOL:

_____

**BEST PERFORMANCE
(GAME, PLAY, CONCERT):**

_____

REPLICATION NATION

Are you a super cartoonist? Let's see your talent!

Copy each Big Nate drawing in the boxes below!

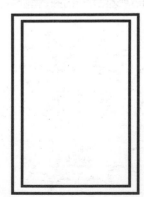

WORST WEEK EVER!

Nate is having one very bad week – check out his lowlights! Ugh, cavities AND a pink uniform? Describe your WORST WEEK EVER, one day at a time:

MONDAY:

TUESDAY:

WEDNESDAY:

THURSDAY:

FRIDAY:

SATURDAY AND SUNDAY?

YAY! IT'S THE WEEKEND!

TRENDSETTER

Nate's started some fun and kind of wacky trends at his school, like hitting his head with a plastic bottle and doodling on his sneakers.

DRAW YOUR FAVOURITE TRENDS:

COOLEST SNEAKERS

CRAZIEST HAIRSTYLE

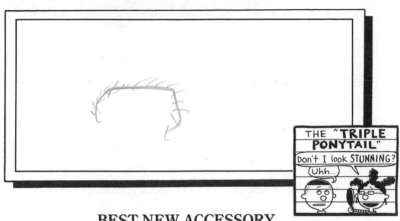

BEST NEW ACCESSORY

MOST AWESOME OUTFIT

TAKE A SHOT!

Coach John is the master of basketball. He's challenging Nate to make one tough shot. Can he do it? Solve the puzzle and help Nate make a basket!

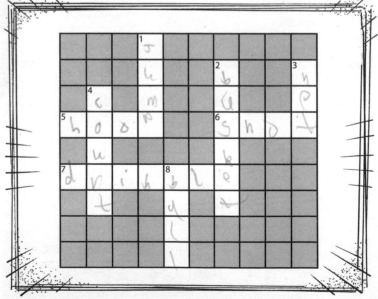

CLUES

ACROSS

5. Circular, rhymes with "soup."

6. Take a _____! Rhymes with "hot."

7. A basketball word for "bounce." Rhymes with "nibble."

DOWN

1. Rhymes with "lump." This makes you shoot higher!

2. This could also be where the Easter Bunny puts his eggs.

3. A fish might get caught in this.

4. Where the game is played; this has wood floors.

8. Rhymes with "hall." Shoot it!

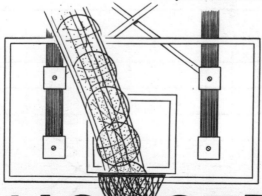

SHOOOFF!

BIRD FOOD

Nate can't handle it! They're replacing all the snacks in the school vending machine with "bird food." Ugh!

LIST THE TOP 20 WORST SNACKS HERE!

1.
2.
3.
4. broccoli
5.
6.
7.
8.
9. kale chips
10.
11.
12.

ANSWER KEY

POP QUIZ PARTY! (pp. 1–2)
1. (b) Kim Cressly
2. (d) Nick Blonsky
3. (c) flute
4. (c) Gina's Geniuses
5. (d) get a C on his homework
Bonus Points! (c) neat
Semaphore: Will you get an A?

WALK THE PLANK (pp. 6–7)

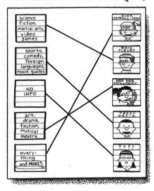

NAME THAT BRAIN! (p. 8)

SLAM DUNK (p. 12)

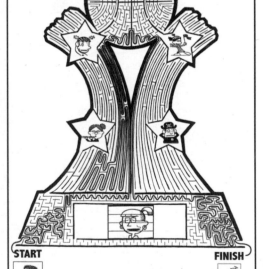

DRESS TO IMPRESS (pp. 14–15)

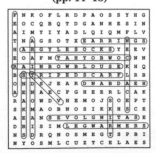

SHORTCUT! (p. 22)
Semaphore:
Run, Nate!

PROBLEM PICS (p.23)

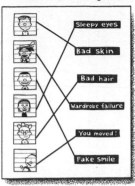

Sleepy eyes
Bad skin
Bad hair
Wardrobe failure
You moved!
Fake smile

YOU'RE AN ACE! (pp. 26–27)

S	H	D	C
D	C	H	S
C	D	S	H
H	S	C	D

MASTERMIND MATCHUP (p. 28)

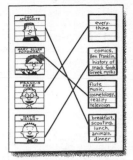

Semaphore: Who will win?

COME **STRAIGHT HOME** AFTER SCHOOL!

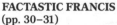

FACTASTIC FRANCIS (pp. 30–31)

1. (c) learning new trivia
2. (d) Captain Tidypants
3. (c) cat
4. (d) no siblings. He's an only child.
5. (b) ironing his tube socks
6. (b) an epidemiologist

KNOCKOUT NOTES (pp. 32–33)

Semaphore: Randy is a moron!

GUESS WHO? (pp. 34–35)

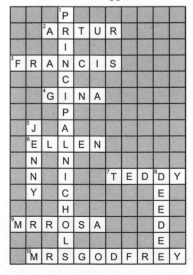

SUPER SPY (p. 36)

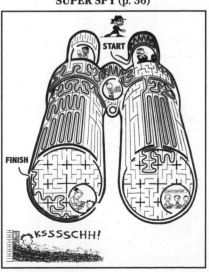

KSSSSCHH!

THINKING CAPS (pp. 42–43)

BRAIN BOWL
(pp. 44–45)
1. North America
2. Spider
3. Saturn
4. Butterfly
5. Japan
6. Heart
7. Triangle
8. Oxygen
9. Atlantic, Pacific, Indian, Arctic, Southern
10. New York

FUNKY FITNESS
(pp. 46–47)

D	M	C	F
C	F	M	D
F	C	D	M
M	D	F	C

NATE NERD
(pp. 48–49)

1. True	3. False	5. False
2. False	4. True	6. True

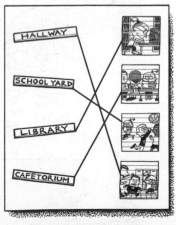

I FOUND THESE OVERDUE LIBRARY BOOKS IN MY ROOM LAST NIGHT.

ROOM RAID (pp. 52–53)

I'VE GOT SOMETHING MORE IMPORTANT TO DO!

Semaphore: Watch out!

SCHOOL SCRAMBLE (p. 54)

HALLWAY
SCHOOL YARD
LIBRARY
CAFETORIUM

IT'S A WONDERFUL LIFE (p. 55)

FINISH

FRANCIS   NATE
BEST FRIENDS

START

PASS THAT CLASS!
(pp. 56–57)

1. (c) Timber Scouts
2. (d) Nick Blonsky
3. (b) Uncle Pedro
4. (d) Dee Dee

Extra Credit!
(b) Mr McTeague

Semaphore:
Get a life, Gina!

READY, SET, CLICK!
(pp. 58–59)

FRANCIS FACTOIDS
(p. 62–63)

C	T	S	O	N	A
O	A	N	S	C	T
N	O	C	A	T	S
T	S	A	N	O	C
A	C	O	T	S	N
S	N	T	C	A	O

WHO'S WHO? (p. 65)

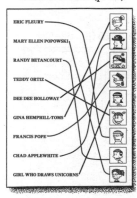

ERIC FLEURY
MARY ELLEN POPOWSKI
RANDY BETANCOURT
TEDDY ORTIZ
DEE DEE HOLLOWAY
GINA HEMPHILL-TOMS
FRANCIS POPE
CHAD APPLEWHITE
GIRL WHO DRAWS UNICORNS

CHEEZ, PLEASE!
(pp. 68–69)

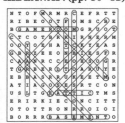

HOUSE OF CARDS
(pp. 72–73)

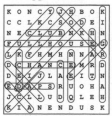

Semaphore:
Lucky you!

HIDEAWAY! (pp. 80–81)

AWKWARD!
(pp. 74–75)
Semaphore:
Uh-oh!

1, 2, 3. . . SNAP! (p. 84)

ODD JOB-A-THON (pp. 88–89)

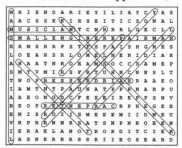

Semaphore: Wow, he can do anything!

YEARBOOK LINEUP (p. 90)

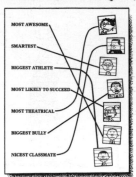

MOST AWESOME
SMARTEST
BIGGEST ATHLETE
MOST LIKELY TO SUCCEED
MOST THEATRICAL
BIGGEST BULLY
NICEST CLASSMATE

ACE PHOTOGRAPHER (p. 91)

START

FINISH

LUCKY CHARMS
(pp. 96–97)

R	H	P	F
P	F	H	R
F	P	R	H
H	R	F	P

MEGA-MESS (pp. 98–99)

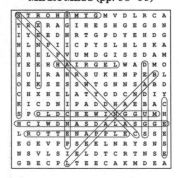

TRIPLE-THREAT TEST (pp. 100–101)

1. (c) Butthurst
2. (b) Luke Warm
3. (c) Gina's Geniuses
4. (d) Mega-Chad
5. (d) Holloway
6. (c) parakeet

LAUGH ATTACK (p. 106)

Semaphores: A bed
Ouch!
The road!

SCHOOL YARD COOL (pp. 118–119)

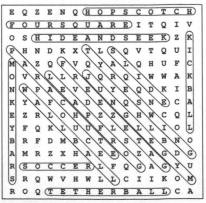

GINA THE GREAT
(pp. 120–121)
1. False   4. True
2. False   5. True
3. True   6. False

NATE-TASTIC TRIVIA
(pp. 126–127)
1. (b) He becomes neat.
2. (b) Nick Blonsky
3. (c) Dorcas
4. (c) Uncle Pedro
5. (d) fleeceball

WHOSE LOCKER IS IT?
(p. 125)

DETECTIVE DEE DEE
(pp. 130–131)

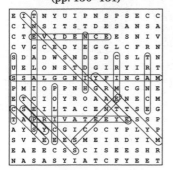

DAD DRAMA
(pp. 138–139)
Semaphore:
So bad!

DANCE FEVER
(pp. 144–145)

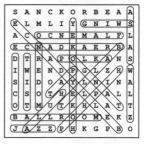

EDITOR-IN-CHIEF (p. 147)

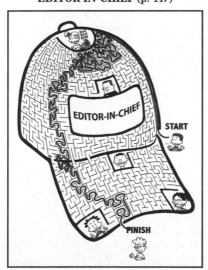

HOOP IT UP! (pp. 148–149)
Semaphore: Watch out, air ball!

ANGER DANGER (p.152)

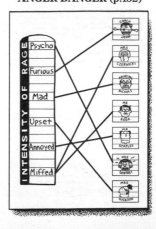

LUCKY CHARMS
(pp. 154–155)
Clover
Rabbit foot
Horseshoe
Star
Rainbow

ON THE SPOT
(pp. 164–165)
1. False
2. False
3. False
4. True
5. True
6. False
7. True
8. False
9. True
10. True
11. False

MASTERMIND
(pp. 170–171)
1. (c) beanbag pellets
2. (d) Mr Rosa
3. (b) Francis and Teddy
4. (b) Randy

HYPNOSIS CENTRAL (p. 172)

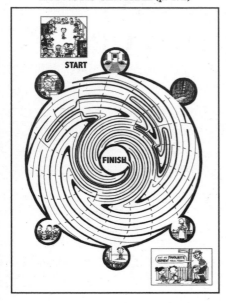

MUSIC MAN (pp. 179–181)

FUNNY BONE (pp. 188–189)
Because it was framed.
Write on!
It overswept!
Stairs.
Crack it up!

TAKE A SHOT! (pp. 202–203)

			¹J					
			U		²B			³N
		⁴C	M		A			E
⁵H	O	O	P		⁶S	H	O	T
		U			K			
⁷D	R	I	B	⁸B	L	E		
		T		A		T		
				L				
				L				

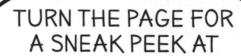

LIVIN' LARGE!

P.S. 38 is pretty small. Everyone knows everyone else. So whenever a new kid shows up, it's a major event. Especially when he's got a name like **THIS**:

Anyway, Principal Nichols asked me to be the kid's "buddy," so it's my job to help him make friends...

...and to show him around the school, which is falling apart. That's what happens when a building is one hundred years old.

Yup, I said one hundred years old. So P.S. 38 is going to throw a gigantic **BIRTHDAY PARTY!**

FUN FACT: A 100TH birthday celebration is called a **CENTENNIAL!**

Actually, Francis, they haven't even decided yet what they're going to call it. But they're promising us plenty of food, fun...

...and the most **EPIC** scavenger hunt in **SCHOOL HISTORY!**

By the way, I've **NEVER** lost a scavenger hunt in my **LIFE!**

"Big Nate is funny, big time."
—Jeff Kinney, author of Diary of a Wimpy Kid

BiG NATE LIVES IT UP

BY NEW YORK TIMES BESTSELLING AUTHOR
Lincoln Peirce

It's *PARTY* TIME!
Read *BIG NATE LIVES IT UP!*

BIG FAN OF BIG NATE?

STILL NEED MORE? BIG NATE HAS ACTIVITIES, DOODLES AND COMICS GALORE!

Lincoln Peirce

(pronounced "purse") is a cartoonist/writer and author of the *New York Times* bestselling Big Nate series, now published in twenty-five countries. He is also the creator of the comic strip *Big Nate*, which appears in more than 250 U.S. newspapers and online daily at www.bignate.com.

Lincoln loves comics, ice hockey, and Cheez Doodles (and dislikes cats, figure skating, and egg salad). Just like Nate.

Check out Big Nate Island at www.poptropica.com. And link to www.bignatebooks.com for more information about the author and the Big Nate series, app, audio and ebooks. Lincoln Peirce lives with his wife and two children in Portland, Maine.